MIDLAND RED IN COLOUR

BERNARD WARR

AMBERLEY

First published 2018

Amberley Publishing
The Hill, Stroud
Gloucestershire, GL5 4EP

www.amberley-books.com

Copyright © Bernard Warr, 2018

The right of Bernard Warr to be identified as
the Author of this work has been asserted in
accordance with the Copyright, Designs and
Patents Act 1988.

ISBN 978 1 4456 7378 3 (print)
ISBN 978 1 4456 7379 0 (ebook)

British Library Cataloguing in Publication Data.
A catalogue record for this book is available from
the British Library.

Typesetting by Amberley Publishing.
Printed in the UK.

Introduction

I grew up in that part of the West Midlands known as the Black Country, encompassing places such as Oldbury, Dudley, Smethwick, Bilston, Cradley Heath, West Bromwich, Walsall and Stourbridge. These were towns where heavy engineering took place, with industries such as iron and steel making, glass foundries, iron smelting, coking, brickworks and coal mining. These produced a high level of atmospheric pollution, turning the outside of buildings black.

Also running through this area, and providing some relief from the drabness with its brightly painted red buses, was an extensive network of stage carriage services provided by the Midland Red or, to give it its 'Sunday Best' title, the Birmingham & Midland Motor Omnibus Company Ltd (BMMO). The bright red buses were seemingly everywhere, taking people to work in the factories, the children to school, mums to the shops and then bringing them all home again. In the 1940s and 1950s, when private car ownership for the working man was almost unheard of, the Midland Red buses set out to satisfy the transport needs of the masses. This involved an extensive fleet of buses and coaches with a network of depots to maintain and crew them.

As I grew up I came to realise just what a major undertaking the BMMO was, covering an area bounded by Nottingham, Leicester, Grantham, Banbury, Evesham, Worcester, Hereford and Shrewsbury with no fewer than thirty-six depots and over 1,700 vehicles.

In the middle of all this was the Carlyle Road Central Works in the Birmingham suburb of Edgbaston, where buses were built, painted and overhauled.

This was the company that I came to work for in August 1960 as the most junior clerk in the Progress Office at Carlyle Works. This workplace gave me access to places that other bus enthusiasts could only dream of. I took a great number of photographs and some of the colour ones are displayed in the pages that follow.

The twenty years before I joined was a time of great innovation by the company under the direction of the new general manager, Donald Sinclair (DMS). He joined the company in 1940 as chief engineer following the retirement of the legendary Mr L. G. Wyndham-Shire. In October 1943, the equally legendary Mr O. C. Power, in whom was vested the overall management of the company, died suddenly and was succeeded by Donald Sinclair as acting general manager. In the summer of the following year he became the permanent general manager.

By the 1950s the company's fortunes were still 'on the up'. The number of passengers carried was increasing each year and would do so until 1954. The fleet was being expanded and modernised, new depots were being opened and others were being extended. The technical superiority of the new buses being introduced was without question, for, in the decade that lay ahead, we were to see lightweight chassisless construction, rubber suspension, disc braking, a fleet of high-speed motorway coaches and an underfloor-engined double-decker.

Despite this optimism, the seeds of change had been sown. The effects of television on people's entertainment habits brought about a reduction in evening and weekend travel, while greater individual prosperity fuelled a rise in private car ownership. By the time the company reached its Golden Jubilee in 1954, bus service passenger numbers had peaked.

The M1 motorway opened on Monday 2 November 1959 and, in what is arguably the company's proudest moment, a fleet of new motorway coaches, the CM5Ts, entered service on that very day, operating the country's first high-speed motorway services between Birmingham and London. The new services enabled the journey time to be cut by two hours to three hours and twenty-five minutes. However, an empty road and no speed limit meant that even these times proved conservative and it became a regular occurrence for coaches to arrive up to forty-five minutes early! To ride on one of these vehicles was a sublime experience. On the motorway, it was constant overtaking; nothing could touch the CM5Ts for speed, and although the speedometers were only calibrated up to 80 mph, the legendary 'ton' was, reportedly, regularly attained.

The company celebrated its Diamond Jubilee on 26 November 1964, but, at the end of 1966, Donald Sinclair retired from his position as general manager after completing twenty-five years of service. There can be little doubt about the sure-footed approach brought to this role by Mr Sinclair. The standards of engineering excellence set by his engineering predecessor, Mr L. G. Wyndham-Shire, were continued and enhanced by his visionary approach. He was succeeded by his deputy, Mr J. W. Womar.

On 14 March 1968 the majority shareholding in the company was sold by British Electric Traction to the Transport Holding Company. Thus, on 1 January 1969, the BMMO became a subsidiary of the National Bus Company.

The period following the sale and Mr Sinclair's departure seemed to coincide with a confused period in the company's history, exemplified by the number of livery variations that were tried out and the decision to cease building their own buses. Many blame this on the takeover by the NBC. Unfortunately, Midland Red had not been able to overcome its engineering staffing problems, resulting in bus production costs rising and the reliability of the fleet falling.

The Transport Act 1968 created the West Midlands Passenger Transport Executive (WMPTE) on 1 October 1969. A duty of the PTE was to come to an agreement with the NBC subsidiary in the area (in this case Midland Red) and British Rail regarding services and fares.

Discussions between the WMPTE and Midland Red took place, culminating in the heads of agreement in June 1973 for WMPTE to take over all Midland Red stage carriage operations in the West Midlands County area. This involved the transfer of 1,396 employees and 413 buses from Midland Red to the WMPTE. The garages at Dudley, Hartshill, Oldbury, Sheepcote Street, Stourbridge and Sutton Coldfield were also transferred. The sale came into effect on 3 December 1973.

Traditionally, the company's marketing had been done on an ad hoc basis. When revenues were high there seemed little need to match income with costs on a route-by-route basis. However, with rampant inflation in the 1970s, something had to be done to stem the losses. The company commissioned consultants to systematically identify those services that could be sustained in the long term at commercially acceptable fare levels. Known initially as the 'Viable Network Project' (VNP), it has now become better known as the Market Analysis Project, or MAP. This produced a host of local service marketing initiatives, each with their own branding, as follows:

'REDDIBUS'	Redditch New Town, March 1976
'AVONBUS'	Stratford-upon-Avon, May 1977
'WAYFARER'	Evesham, July 1977
'WENDAWAY'	Kidderminster, November 1977
'WANDAWARD'	Hereford, March 1978
'TELLUS'	Telford New Town, April 1978
'SEVERNLINK'	Worcester and Bromsgrove, January 1979
'LANCER'	Coalville and Swadlincote, February 1979
'HUNTER'	Nuneaton, May 1979
'MERCIAN'	Tamworth and Lichfield, September 1979
'CHASERIDER'	Cannock and Stafford, May 1980
'LEAMINGTON & WARWICK'	Leamington, May 1980
'HOTSPUR'	Shrewsbury and Ludlow, November 1980
'RUGBY – MIDLAND RED'	Rugby, April 1981
'RIDERCROSS'	Banbury, July 1981

Many of these brandings will be observed on the images from the period.

The shortfall in income for 1981/2 was estimated to be £5 million, and with only £2.5 million of available financial support from county councils, further drastic cuts were needed.

In February 1981, the decision was taken to close Head Office (Midland House), the Divisional Offices and Central Works and to divide the company into four regional bus companies and one coach company, with each county council getting only the level of service for which it was prepared to pay. The administrative and secretarial services previously provided by Midland House and the Divisional Offices would in future be provided by neighbouring NBC companies.

The new Midland Red companies commenced operation on 6 September 1981 and were as follows:

Midland Red (North) Ltd covering the former North West Division, operating 230 vehicles from six garages.
Midland Red (East) Ltd covering the former North East Division and operating 181 vehicles from four garages.
Midland Red (South) Ltd covering the former South East Division and operating 163 vehicles from five garages.

Midland Red (West) Ltd covering the former South West Division and operating 183 vehicles from six garages.
Midland Red (Express) Ltd operating eighty-two coaches from one garage.

The new freedoms available to the operating companies meant many changes to liveries and types of vehicle used. The 1980s saw massive growth in the use of minibuses, some of which are illustrated in the following pages. Many second-hand vehicles were purchased as the needs of the customers ebbed and flowed with the ups and downs of the economy.

The images that follow are arranged in chronological order based on type and the date they entered into the fleet. In addition to my own images and those in my collection from numerous (largely unknown) photographers, I must pay tribute to Chris Aston of Omnicolour and my brother, Stuart Warr, for allowing me to dig freely into their collections of images and publish a selection to make up for the inadequacies of my own collection. I am also indebted to Connor Stait of Amberley Publishing, whose idea it was to compile the volume in the first place. His continued encouragement has been invaluable.

Bernard Warr
Market Rasen, Lincolnshire
February 2018

Where all our bus spotting journeys began... (Bernard Warr)

New in 1934, HA 9483 was fitted with a thirty-eight-seat Short Bros body and a Rolls-Royce petrol engine. In 1938 the petrol engine was changed for a BMMO 'K' type diesel engine and the type code became CON (Converted ONward). Fleet numbers were only carried from 1944, when she became 1532. After a very long service life of twenty-two years, she was withdrawn in 1956 and sold to the City of Birmingham Water Department (whose name can be seen on the side of the vehicle) and based at Rhayader in connection with the Elan Valley dam project. In this role, she lasted until 1968. (Bernard Warr collection)

New in 1937, and fitted with an English Electric thirty-eight-seat body and a BMMO diesel engine, DHA 643 was classified as a SON (Saloon ONward), with the allocated fleet number 2025, in 1944. After nineteen years in service she was withdrawn in 1956 and sold to the City of Birmingham Water Department, based at Rhayader, in 1957. Used for staff transport, she was already showing signs of dereliction when this picture was taken in 1964. Like 1532 she was scrapped in 1968. (Bernard Warr collection)

ONC (ONward Coach) 2286 (FHA 418) was the last of its type to remain in service and was kept for special duties, such as when local football teams needed to parade around their home towns in celebration of a victory. This was achieved by putting a platform over the front seats and opening the very large sun roof so that players could stand on the platform with their upper bodies projecting up through the roof and wave to the crowds. New in 1939, 2286 was finally withdrawn in 1963. Although sold for preservation in 1964, this was not successful, and she was scrapped in 1970. (Bernard Warr)

FEDD 2254 (FHA 236). The FEDD was the mainstay of the Midland Red double-deck fleet from 1934 until the late 1940s. Bodywork was by BMMO (1), Short Bros (50), MCCW (135) and Brush (150). The first 186 were fitted from new with petrol engines and the MCCW variants were converted to diesel engines in the late 1940s. This image of 2254, a diesel variant dating from 1938, was taken in Stourbridge in the summer of 1960, and clearly shows the wide entrance and the manually operated doors that could be closed to keep the weather out. Withdrawal came in December 1960. (Bernard Warr collection)

Another image of FEDD 2254 in Stourbridge, this time showing the off-side. Note the fuel tank under the driver's seat! This was not too bad in the diesel version shown here, but for the earlier petrol-engined versions it must have been a little hazardous if the driver liked to smoke. (Bernard Warr collection)

Another FEDD seeing out its days at Stourbridge depot in 1960. 2232 (FHA 214), also new in 1938, spent most of its life in Worcestershire with long periods at both Worcester and Kidderminster depots. It was withdrawn from Stourbridge depot in November 1960. (Bernard Warr collection)

Type SOS 'SON' (Saloon **ON**ward) 2418 (GHA 337). New in June 1940 with bodywork by Brush, it was withdrawn in March 1958 and sold to a showman shortly afterwards. The next fifteen years saw a gradual decline and by 1983 it was derelict. Fortunately, it was acquired for preservation by the embryonic Wythall Museum in that year. Restoration priorities and shortage of funding meant that thirty years were to pass before 2418 could take to the road again in the fully restored condition seen here. (Bernard Warr collection)

A further view of 2418 at the Wythall Museum with the restoration almost complete in October 2001 – an absolute credit to all who worked on her. (Stuart Warr)

On a summer's morning in May 1963, S6 3038 stands in St Margaret's bus station, Leicester, awaiting its next turn of duty. New in April 1947 with MCCW bodywork, 3038 was a long-term resident of Leicester's Sandacre Street depot from July 1949 until withdrawal in March 1964. (Chris Aston/Omnicolour)

AD2 3192 (JHA 93) is seen in Leicester's St Margaret's bus station on a cold but sunny day in January 1961. 3192 was a MCCW-bodied version, new in April 1950, and after spells at Oldbury and Hinckley depots moved to Leicester Sandacre Street in May 1958, where it remained until withdrawn in November 1961. (Peter Smith/Omnicolour)

3311 (KHA 311) shows off the stylish lines of the BMMO-designed Duple body. She was allocated for most of her working life to Southgate Street Garage, Leicester, before withdrawal in April 1962. At this point a new career beckoned as a dual-control driver training vehicle, which was a role she fulfilled until April 1975. Preservation followed in 1980. (Stuart Warr)

The nearside view of 3311, showing the graceful lines of the Duple body. (Bernard Warr)

At a time when most coach builders were producing half-cab vehicles, the striking good looks of the C1 front must have caused quite a stir. This is 3301 (KHA 301), which was new in November 1948. She served at several depots, including Digbeth and Leicester, before withdrawal in May 1963. Like 3311 she was also retained for further duties and, after being reseated to C24C, became the transport for the Midland Red Concert Orchestra, continuing in this role until she was sold for preservation in February 1971. (Bernard Warr)

The two preserved C1s, side by side at the Wythall Museum in October 2008. (Stuart Warr)

Photographed in April 1961, C2 touring coach 3356 (KHA 356) is in Central Works following a pre-season check prior to its return to Bearwood depot for the 1961 season. This was to be the last year that C2s were used on the company's prestigious Coach Cruises, their role being taken over by the Plaxton-bodied CL2s in 1962. All the C2s had been withdrawn by the end of 1966.

Seen in June 1962 on the bus park behind Digbeth depot is S8 3253 (JHA 853) . 3253 spent the whole of its working life based at Digbeth depot, from August 1948 until July 1963. In common with other members of its class and the S6s, the length was increased to 29 feet 3 inches between 1951 and 1953 by Charles H. Roe of Leeds, and she was upseated to forty-four. (Bernard Warr)

Open-platformed D5 3457 (MHA 457) awaits her next turn of duty outside Wigston depot on a sunny afternoon in May 1961. This vehicle was the first of its type to be introduced and was sent new to Bearwood depot in July 1949. She came to Wigston in October 1957 and remained there for the rest of her days, until she was withdrawn in July 1964. (Bernard Warr)

D5B 3856 (NHA 856) departs The Newarke bus station in Leicester on route L1 on a sunny afternoon in May 1964. Although fitted with driver-controlled passenger doors, it was quite common to see them left open in warm weather. Passengers were quite used to taking their lives in their own hands and jumping on and off the bus while it was moving. I think people found being confined to boarding and alighting only at bus stops a bit restrictive! 3856 was new in September 1951 and was withdrawn from service in March 1966. (Martin Llewellyn/Omnicolour)

A sister D5B, 3854 (NHA 854), this time photographed in March 1965 in Watergate Lane, Leicester, and heading for The Newarke on service L22. Despite the dry day the bus shows signs of recent bad weather and is in need of a good wash. 3854 was new in August 1951 and was withdrawn from service in December 1966. (Martin Llewellyn/Omnicolour)

Two D5Bs parked up in Hinckley awaiting their next turn of duty in the summer of 1964. 3837 was new in June 1951, and after a couple of years working from Digbeth depot moved to Hinckley, remaining there until withdrawal in October 1966. 3781 was new in November 1950 and didn't find its way to Hinckley until 1958, remaining there until withdrawal in October 1964. (Peter Smith/Omnicolour)

I'm not sure what the collective noun for D5s is, but there must a coven (or a gaggle, or a swarm) on display here outside Oldbury garage at Birchley Crossing in June 1960. (Bernard Warr)

Almost at the end of its working life, GD6 3575 (MHA 75) leaves Dudley bus station on route D1 in March 1962. For thirteen years, these very conventional 1940s buses had provided services in and around Dudley. 3575 lasted just another six months after this picture was taken, being withdrawn in September 1962. (Chris Aston/Omnicolour)

Awaiting its next turn of duty in Dudley bus station we find GD6 3562 (MHA 62) on a sunny day in April 1962. All of the class had been withdrawn by the end of 1962, 3562 succumbing in November. (Chris Aston/Omnicolour)

This October 2012 view of 3744 (NHA 744) was taken shortly after its full and comprehensive restoration at the Wythall Museum. Of note is the use of the original 'lined out' livery, complete with black-painted wheel valances. (Stuart Warr)

Contrast this picture with the previous one of 3744. Here she is seen in the semi-derelict state that the restorers were faced with when she arrived at the museum in 1981. 3744 was new in October 1950 and became a long-term resident at Sutton Coldfield depot. After thirteen years in Sutton she was moved to Stourbridge depot, from where she was withdrawn in September 1964. The following month she was purchased by the Automotive Products Group and converted to a mobile research unit, based at AP's Shenington test area. In 1981 AP approached the newly established Wythall Museum and offered a transfer for preservation. This was accepted and 3744 arrived in August 1981. (Bernard Warr collection)

A photograph taken in 2005 showing progress with the restoration. These were the last single-deckers to be produced by the company where the driver had an enclosed cab and an external door. The door to the passenger saloon can be seen in the closed position. When opened, it folded back against the driver's cab; this was very good for ventilation on a hot summer's day, but most of the rest of the year passengers preferred it to be closed! (Bernard Warr)

3744 heads out from the Wythall Museum for a trip to the Maypole and back in the autumnal sunshine of an October day in 2012. (Stuart Warr)

S13 Mk II 3950 (OHA 950) stands in St Margaret's bus station, Leicester, in May 1964. 3950 was allocated to Leicester Sandacre Street depot for most of its life, apart from a six-month spell at Wigston before withdrawal in August 1966. The more comfortable semi-coach seats can be clearly seen in this view. (Chris Aston/Omnicolour)

LD8 4013 (SHA 413) waits in Leicester Southgate Street bus station for her return working to Birmingham on the X68 service. 4013 was a Digbeth vehicle at this time, having previously worked for Ludlow and Wolverhampton depots. Note the un-lined all-over red livery applied to this vehicle, which was common from the late 1950s onwards and was a cost-saving measure. 4013 was new in February 1953, and was withdrawn from the Leicester area engineering float in March 1967. (Chris Aston/Omnicolour)

LD8 4031 (SHA 431) was the only example of the class to survive into preservation. New in March 1953, she spent the whole of her working life based at Digbeth depot, being withdrawn in May 1967. Shortly afterwards she was sold to Foster Brothers, the Birmingham men's outfitters, for use as staff transport. This role came to an end in July 1971 and she was acquired for preservation. Changes of ownership followed and in June 1977 she became the property of the '1685 Group', who commenced a long and very thorough restoration that was not finished until 2010. She is seen here departing the Wythall Museum for the Maypole in October 2012. (Stuart Warr)

LD8 4031 at Bewdley railway station on the Severn Valley Railway in September 2010. Note the livery has reverted to the full 1953 version with black valances and yellow lining out. (Stuart Warr)

D7 4730 (730 BHA) is shown working the 590 service from Coventry to Stratford-upon-Avon. The location is believed to be in the region of the Pool Meadow bus station in Coventry. New in February 1957 to Leamington depot, she remained there for all her service life, being withdrawn in December 1971. (Arnold Richardson/Omnicolour)

D7 4759 (759 BHA) turns round in Evesham High Street working local service E3 on 13 July 1967. 4759 was allocated to Evesham depot from new in June 1957 and remained there until September 1969. (Bernard Warr collection)

D7 4740 (740 BHA) is seen turning into St Peters Hill, Grantham, after leaving the bus station in April 1965, returning to Leicester on route 662. Grantham was about as far east, on stage carriage services, as Midland Red ran. 4740 was new to Southgate Street depot in Leicester in March 1957 and spent her whole service life there until she was withdrawn in February 1971. (Bernard Warr collection)

Another picture of a D7, 4759, from 13 July 1967, heading outward from the High Street towards the River Avon bridge and into the Eastfield housing estate. (Bernard Warr collection)

D7 4482 (XHA 482) was from the third batch and was new to Ludlow depot in March 1956. After a year at Ludlow she was transferred to Digbeth and remained there for four years. She then moved to Stourbridge for a further six years before being withdrawn from Hinckley at the end of 1971. She was sold to Aston Martin at Newport Pagnell, who kept her until February 1977, when she moved in to preservation. This photo was taken at the Wythall Museum on 12 October 2008 and shows the original livery to good effect. (Bernard Warr)

S14 4255 (UHA 255) entered service from Worcester depot on 8 April 1955. In March 1963 it was moved to Leamington and remained there until July 1967, when it returned to Worcestershire – this time at the small Malvern garage. By now a candidate for retirement, it moved often between Hereford and Worcester garages until early in 1968, when, surprisingly, it returned to works for overhaul. This decision was even more surprising because 4255 was one of relatively few S14s not to be converted to driver-only operation. The reprieved 4255 was used as a float vehicle and operated from Malvern, Worcester, Redditch, Kidderminster and Bromsgrove garages before finally returning to Worcester depot, from where it was withdrawn in November 1970. It is seen here in October 2001, in the condition it was in at the end of its working life and before any restoration had taken place. It has since been cosmetically restored. (Stuart Warr)

S14 4564 (564 AHA) stands alongside S15 4640 (640 AHA) in the car park at Carlyle Works in May 1961. 4564 was a Hereford vehicle for the whole of its service life, from July 1956 until withdrawn in November 1970. S15 4640 was allocated to Dudley depot at this time. (Bernard Warr)

S14 4709 (709 BHA) is seen on Evesham High Street on 13 July 1967 working local service E5. Nowadays the cream-painted building is a Coral Bookmaker's shop and the white-painted building on the extreme left is 'The Olde Lambe Inne'. (Bernard Warr collection)

S15 4613 (613 AHA) is seen parked up on the Digbeth depot bus park, awaiting its next turn of duty on 18 July 1963. 4613 was new to Digbeth in June 1957 and was converted to one-man operation (OMO) in January 1966. As can be seen, litter was as much a problem in 1963 as it is now! (Bernard Warr)

C3 4240 (UHA 240) is seen in Victoria Coach Station in London on a rather murky day in April 1961, having worked down from Birmingham on the service via Daventry and Stony Stratford. 4240 was allocated to Sheepcote Street depot in Birmingham from new and, apart from short spells at Evesham and Oldbury, remained there until withdrawn in March 1966. (Bernard Warr)

C4 4250 is seen in the Carlyle Works car park in April 1961 following its pre-season preparation. The differences between the C3 and C4 can be clearly seen in this photograph. 4250 was about to be allocated to Sandacre Street depot, Leicester, for the 1961 season, although, with this exception, it had been a Worcester depot coach for most of its working life. Withdrawal came in March 1966. (Bernard Warr)

C5 4818 (818 HHA) was new in April 1961 and spent most of her operational life at Kidderminster depot. Seen here in about 1962 on a day tour in the company of sister C5, 4820 (820 HHA) of Cradley Heath depot. Both were converted to C5A in the summer of 1966 and lasted until 1971. (Arnold Richardson/Omnicolour)

C5A 4788 (788 GHA) was converted from a conventional C5 in July 1966, and at the time of this picture was working from Stourbridge depot. The inward-opening power door can be discerned. Despite the conversion and the non-coach livery, 4788 is seen here actually working a coach service to Cheltenham! In January 1970, she was converted for OMO and was withdrawn at the end of November. (Arnold Richardson/Omnicolour)

Ex-Kemp & Shaw Leyland PD2/12 JBC 989, fleet number 4845, is seen operating Leicester local service L89 in June 1962, surrounded by Midland Red 'homegrown' vehicles. 4845 was new in 1952 and was withdrawn in May 1967. (Chris Aston/Omnicolour)

Two D9s under construction outside the erecting shop in February 1961. The one without paneling is 4920, and is awaiting entry to the bodywork erecting shop. The one with paneling has just come out of the erecting shop and will shortly be taken to the paint spray booth for painting. (Bernard Warr)

Almost completed 4927 (927 KHA) waits on the Carlyle Works car park for its fleet name and numbers to be applied before starting its service life at Stourbridge Garage in June 1961. Note the illuminated advertising sign between the upper and lower decks. These were a popular innovation at the time but, as one or two unfortunate drivers found out, leaving them lit up after the engine was stopped could result in battery drain and an inability to restart the engine! (Bernard Warr)

D9 4948 (2948 HA), working service 120 from Langley, unloads passengers at the Birmingham Museum & Art Gallery in Victoria Square before moving round to Paradise Street to reload on 22 September 1962. New the previous December, 4948 spent the whole of its service life at Oldbury Garage, being withdrawn in December 1973. (Bernard Warr collection)

D9 4997 (2997 HA) is seen in Broad Street, Birmingham, while approaching the Hall of Memory with service 130 from Stourbridge. The date is May 1972 and the following December she would pass to the West Midlands Passenger Transport Executive (WMPTE) after the takeover of her home garage, Stourbridge. She was withdrawn in April 1974 and was scrapped by Birds at Stratford in July 1975. (Arnold Richardson/ Omnicolour)

D9 4903 (903 KHA). New in January 1961 she was allocated to Redditch Garage and remained there for five years until she moved on to Nuneaton at the end of 1966. Just over five years later she was moved to Wigston, from where she was withdrawn in December 1974. Almost immediately she was purchased by Prince Marshall (Obsolete Fleet), London, and given the fleet number OM1. After conversion to open top (as seen here) she was used for London sightseeing tours until the end of 1983. At this point she was sold to Mauritius Brauerei GmbH (Mehnert Promotion), Zwickau, Germany, and was re-registered V JM 41H. She was repainted into overall blue livery and used as a promotional vehicle. In 2001 a further overhaul and repaint into green livery took place and the promotional use continued at least until 2005. (Bernard Warr collection)

D9 5026 (3026 HA) is seen in February 1973 on service 144 in Newport Street bus station, Worcester, having worked from Birmingham and going forward to Malvern Wells. 5026 was new in January 1963 and spent many years working from Stourbridge garage until a move to Worcester garage came in May 1971. Withdrawal came three years later and she was purchased by Ensign Bus and placed on a two-year contract with Lesney Toys. A further sale to St Ferdinand Vins Français, London, as NW5, saw her acting as a mobile wine tasting vehicle. After a year she was sold again to Pieroth Ltd and became a playbus in a vineyard in Uckfield by September 1982. (Bernard Warr collection)

An immaculate D9 5039 (3039 HA) is captured in 1972 in Charles Street, Leicester, working local service L8 to South Wigston. Note the blanked-out illuminated advertisement sign between the floors and the later style fleet name and numbering just prior to the National Bus Company period. 5039 spent all of her twelve-year life at Wigston garage, being withdrawn in May 1975. (Arnold Richardson/Omnicolour)

D9 5314 (6314 HA) looks in a rather sorry state, having been stripped of fleet name, numbers and BMMO insignia badge on the radiator grill. She had been sold to Marshall (Obsolete Fleet) in June 1980, hence the removal of all markings. Marshall's allocated her the number OM10, but eventually chose not to convert her to open top and offered her for sale again. In October 1981 she was purchased by Peter Hudd, Eltham, for preservation and in the image above she is seen with preserved S23 5919 on 12 September 1982. (Bernard Warr collection)

D9 5332 (6332 HA) is seen on a wet day passing Stafford railway station in about 1976. Note the NBC livery complete with grey wheels. 5332 had a fourteen-year service life, which was all spent at Stafford garage, ending in July 1977. (Bernard Warr collection)

An immaculate D9 5342 is seen visiting the Wythall Transport Museum on 14 October 2007. New to Stourbridge garage in September 1963, she remained there all her working life, being taken over by WMPTE with the rest of the garage in December 1973. She was sold into preservation when withdrawn in October 1977, and, having passed through a variety of owners, is now resident at the Black Country Museum in Dudley. (Bernard Warr)

Another view of D9 5342, in the company of Daimler DD13 5225 and Leicester City Leyland Titan PD3 TBC 164. (Bernard Warr collection)

A rather dirty D9 5362 (6362 HA) is seen in St Margaret's bus station, Leicester, in about 1965. (Bernard Warr collection)

D9 5399 pauses alongside the village pond in Main Street, Willersey, opposite the Bell Hotel. New in July 1965, she spent most of her working life at garages around the Black Country, until February 1976, when a spell in Leicestershire began. This ended when she was withdrawn in March 1980 and put into store. Reinstated in July 1982, she went on loan to Cannock garage for two years before being loaned to the BaMMOT at Wythall Museum in June 1984. She became a permanent resident in October 1992. (Bernard Warr collection)

High up in the Malvern Hills at Malvern Wells is the southern terminus of the 144 service, where buses had to be turned round in this recess cut out of the hillside. With a bus the size of a D9, shown here, careful co-operation between the driver, the conductor and his whistle was called for! (Bernard Warr collection)

Midland Red D9 5405 (EHA 405D) has been nicely turned round at Malvern and is ready to start its journey to Birmingham on service 144 in July 1975. Although allocated to Bearwood garage from new in 1966, 5405 was sent to Malvern garage in May 1973, where she remained until the garage closed on 2 October 1976. Withdrawal came a month later. (Bernard Warr collection)

D9 5415 (EHA 415D) is seen here being operated by Wheels of Nuneaton, an organisation set up by Ashley Wakelin to capture the bus driver experience market together with more conventional operations like weddings and other forms of private hire work. 5415 was photographed at a rally at the Wythall Transport Museum in July 1995. (Bernard Warr)

Ten years have passed between this image and the previous one, but the return to the traditional Midland Red livery is a welcome sight! 5415 is still engaged in driver experience and private hire work for Wheels of Nuneaton, and was photographed at a rally on 31 July 2005. (Bernard Warr)

Another photograph of D9 5415, this time seen arriving at Kidderminster railway station on 11 October 1998. 5415 was new to Kidderminster garage in February 1966 and remained there until March 1973, when a transfer to Tamworth garage took place. Withdrawal from there occurred in September 1977. A variety of owners followed before she was acquired by Ashley Wakelin for the Wheels company. Consequent upon Ashley's retirement the ownership of 5415 has now passed to the Big Red Bus Co., Liverpool. (Stuart Warr)

D9 5424 is seen arriving at Kidderminster railway station on 1 October 2000. Now part of Roger Burdett's fleet, she was new to Wolverhampton garage in April 1966, and after spells at Dudley, Kidderminster and Stafford, was withdrawn in July 1977. (Stuart Warr)

D10 4943 (943 KHA) loads passengers in Stafford for town service S93 in September 1969. (Martin Llewellyn/Omnicolour)

D10 4943 out and about in the rural West Midlands in July 2005. (Bernard Warr)

4943 takes centre stage at a
Wythall Museum open day in
October 2008. (Bernard Warr)

4943 lines up with a preserved C1, 3301, at the Wythall Transport Museum in July 2005 (Bernard Warr)

CL3 4207 (UHA 207), allocated to Oldbury garage, stands on the quayside in Ilfracombe in June 1962, showing off the all-over light stone livery, which is relieved only by the colour of the fleet name. (Bernard Warr)

CL3 4220 (UHA 220), from Digbeth Garage, loads passengers in Bearwood bus station in July 1963. Note the reinstatement of the black and red coach livery apart from the light stone band around the waistline. (Bernard Warr)

CL3 4203 (UHA 203) of Dudley garage is seen on a Scottish tour in August 1964, passing the Forth Rail and Road bridges. (Martin Llewellyn/Omnicolour)

CL3 4226 (UHA 226), from Bearwood Garage, is also on a Scottish tour in 1964, and is seen at Fort William. Note that the light stone band is now confined to the sides of the vehicle. (Chris Aston/Omnicolour)

5073 in service at Wythall Museum on an open day in October 2007. Having just discharged her passengers, she is about to cross over to the departure stand to begin another tour. (Bernard Warr collection)

S15 5073 (5073 HA) is seen undertaking an afternoon tour in post-preservation times. 5073 was new to Shrewsbury garage in November 1962 and remained there for the whole of her working life, being withdrawn in September 1974. She moved in to preservation in early 1975 and is now owned by Wythall Transport Museum. (Bernard Warr collection)

On 12 October 2008, S15 5073 awaits its next turn of duty adjacent to a typical rudimentary bus shelter, so beloved of the BMMO, together with the company's adaptation of a Birmingham City Transport bus stop sign. (Stuart Warr)

S15 5056 (5056 HA) arrives at Kidderminster railway station on 14 October 2001. The red pillars and the revised bodyside trim can be clearly seen. 5056 was new to Hereford garage in August 1962, and after spells at Digbeth, Kidderminster, Sutton Coldfield and Coalville, was withdrawn in October 1972. In the next thirteen years, she worked for three separate contractors before becoming transport for the Melton Mowbray Crusaders' Boys Club in 1977. She entered preservation in 1982, and since 2003 has been part of Roger Burdett's collection. (Stuart Warr)

The very last S16 to be constructed, 5545 is seen here arriving at Kidderminster railway station on 14 October 2001. She was new to Coalville garage in July 1964, and after spells at Stafford and Leamington, was withdrawn from service in July 1976. She moved immediately into preservation and is now owned by the Wythall Transport Museum. (Stuart Warr)

S16 5545 rests in the autumn sun at the Wythall Transport Museum on 28 October 2001. (Stuart Warr)

A rather travel-weary S17 5460 (460 HA) is seen shortly after her transfer to Sandacre Street garage in Leicester in February 1970. 5460 was always a Leicester area vehicle, starting life in October 1963 at Sandacre Street followed by short spells at Southgate Street and Nuneaton garages. In September 1969, she was converted to OMO prior to the move back to Sandacre Street, and it was from here that she was withdrawn in October 1976. (Bernard Warr collection)

S17 5479 is seen on the cobbles outside Kidderminster railway station on 14 October 2001. New to Coalville Garage in January 1964, she spent all of her working life in the Leicestershire area. Withdrawn in November 1979, she was acquired for preservation by the forerunners of the Worcester Bus Preservation Society, and is currently kept at the Aldridge Transport Museum. (Stuart Warr)

S17 5616 stands in Nuneaton bus station, ready for her next outing on local service N34 in July 1970. The conversion to OMO will be noted. 5616 worked for a number of garages in her time but was finally withdrawn from Hinckley in November 1976. (Bernard Warr collection)

S17 5699 (CHA 699C) makes her way out of Cheltenham on service 373 to Worcester. This image, captured in March 1977, was taken well in to the NBC era, as can be seen from the livery changes. 5699 was new in September 1965 and had been allocated first to Nuneaton depot, and had also seen service at Evesham, Malvern, Shrewsbury, Stafford and finally Worcester a month before this picture was taken. She was to last only another few months, being withdrawn in July 1977. (Bernard Warr collection)

S17 5749 (EHA 749D) makes her way gingerly through the snow at Kilby Bridge in February 1969 on service 562 to Welford. 5749 was based at Southgate Street, Leicester, for the whole of her working life, which came to an end in May 1977. (Chris Aston/Omnicolour)

S17 5767 (EHA 767D) arrives at Kidderminster railway station, 1 October 2000. This vehicle was new to Sandacre Street garage in Leicester in September 1966 and after about a year was transferred to Wigston garage. The next twelve years were spent here until withdrawal came in September 1979. A move into preservation came soon afterwards, and it is now in the ownership of the Wythall Transport Museum. (Stuart Warr)

LS18 5147 (5147 HA) is seen making its way through the Cotswold village of Chipping Campden on 21 May 1977 while working for Evesham garage. New to Nuneaton garage in December 1962, she had already worked for Rugby garage and been loaned to Potteries Motor Traction before coming to Evesham in March 1976. A move to Hinckley came in July 1978, from where she was withdrawn in January 1979. (Bernard Warr collection)

On a sunny May 1963 morning, an almost brand-new, dual-purpose LS18A, 5180 (5180 HA), departs Southgate Street bus station, Leicester, to return to her home depot at Hereford on the long X91 service. (Chris Aston/Omnicolour)

LS18 5236 (5236 HA) is seen on the Parade in Leamington in March 1965, working local service L43. 5236 was a Leamington vehicle for most of her working life, moving to Hinckley in May 1977, from where she was withdrawn at the end of 1978. Among the shops can be seen the offices of the Leamington Building Society, which was taken over by the Bradford & Bingley BS, and, when that organisation succumbed to the financial crisis in 2008, was then taken over by Santander. Nothing is forever! (Martin Llewellen/Omnicolour)

On 14 July 1963, DD11 5273 is parked up in Birchall Street, which is close to Digbeth garage in Birmingham. At the time of the photograph, 5273 was barely two months old and was to remain at Digbeth for four years before being transferred to Sutton Coldfield. In 1973 she was loaned to and then sold to City of Oxford Motor Services, becoming their fleet number 909 in February 1975. Just over a year later she was sold to the Bristol Omnibus Company for spares. (Bernard Warr)

CM6T 5656 (BHA 656C) was the only vehicle of this type to survive into preservation. She was new in September 1965 and worked for Bearwood garage for the whole of her service life (apart from a few months at Cradley Heath before withdrawal in September 1974). She is now preserved in full working order at the Wythall Transport Museum, where she was photographed in October 2008. (Stuart Warr)

Another view of 5656, full of enthusiastic passengers and departing the Wythall Museum on 14 October 2012. (Bernard Warr)

S21 5864 (JHA 864E) is seen at Evesham on 13 July 1967 preparing to undertake a private hire duty. Note the maroon-coloured roof and then wonder about change for change's sake! At this date, she was less than two weeks old and was to remain an Evesham vehicle for six years when a move to Redditch took place. Two years later a final move to Wellington occurred, and it was from here that she was withdrawn and scrapped in May 1980. (Bernard Warr collection)

S21 5861 (JHA 861E) is photographed working the S25 town service in Shrewsbury on 3 September 1974. By comparing this image with the previous one of 5864, some changes are worth commenting on. From 1970 onwards the whole batch was converted to OMO and the two-tone dual purpose livery has been replaced by NBC poppy red. The rather attractive raised aluminium fleet names from the side and front have also gone. 5861 entered service on 23 May 1967 at Shrewsbury depot and remained there for over nine years, before moving to Wellington depot at the end of 1976 and Swadlincote two years later. Withdrawal came in June 1979, when she was sold for scrap. (Bernard Warr collection)

S22 5901 (MHA 901F) is seen here at a rally at the Wythall Transport Museum in October 2008. She was new to Worcester in July 1968 and remained there for nearly eleven years before moving to Hinckley at the beginning of 1979. A short spell at Leamington followed in 1980 and she was withdrawn in September 1980. Preservation followed, and since October 1988 she has been in the ownership of the Worcester Bus Preservation Society. (Stuart Warr)

S22 5905 (PHA 505G) arrives at a rally at Kidderminster station on 11 October 1998. When new at the end of July 1968, 5905 was allocated to Banbury garage. A move to Nuneaton came at the end of 1971, from where she was withdrawn in June 1980. In September, 5905 was acquired by Derbyshire Constabulary, who retained ownership until April 1982, when a move into preservation took place. She is now owned by the Leicester Transport Heritage Trust. The black and red coach livery seen here was never carried during her time with Midland Red. (Stuart Warr)

S23 5919 (RHA 919G), one of the last vehicles to be wholly built by Carlyle Works, is seen in October 2008 in NBC livery, complete with grey wheels. New in December 1968, she joined the Banbury garage fleet and moved to Malvern in September 1971. Five years later a move to Wellington occurred, and it was from here that she was withdrawn in July 1980. She has, by a variety of organisations, been in preservation ever since, and is currently owned by the Leicester Transport Heritage Trust. (Stuart Warr)

S23 5921 (RHA 921G) demonstrates the decline in standards of presentation and maintenance that the NBC-owned Midland Red had suffered. At this time, believed to be late 1979, she was still a Wigston garage vehicle and had been from being new in January 1969. The location is St Margaret's bus station in Leicester. A transfer to Leamington took place in May 1980, from where she was withdrawn in October of that year and sold for scrap. (Bernard Warr collection)

S23 5956 (UHA 956H) is seen having been restored to NBC Midland Red livery with Wendaway branding. She is now owned by the Wythall Transport Museum and seen here at one of their open days in July 2005. 5956 was new to Kidderminster garage in November 1969 and remained there for the whole of her service life, until she was withdrawn in January 1981. (Stuart Warr)

S23 5963 stands with DD12 6015, both awaiting restoration in about 1985. The image has been included to show how paintwork deteriorates after continual exposure to the weather. (Bernard Warr collection)

S23 5963 (UHA 963) after restoration to NBC Midland Red livery with Hunter branding. At the time of this photograph (14 October 2007) she was being operated by Wheels of Nuneaton, mostly on private hire work, under the banner of 'Midland Red Coaches'. She was new to Rugby garage in December 1969 and remained there for all of her stage carriage working life until moved to Nuneaton one month before withdrawal in November 1980. Alongside 5963 is sister S23 5981, restored to WMPTE livery. (Bernard Warr)

DD12 6015 is seen at the Wythall Transport Museum open day on 12 October 2008. Originally allocated to Kidderminster garage from (almost) new in December 1966 (her first month in service was at Leamington garage), she moved on to Worcester in June 1969. A five-year spell at Evesham began in March 1970. After short spells at Worcester, Evesham, Tamworth and Coalville, she passed to Midland Red (East) on its formation in September 1981, remaining at Coalville before withdrawal from there at the end of 1983. She was quickly acquired for preservation and is now owned by the Wythall Transport Museum. (Bernard Warr collection)

DD12 6044 (JHA 44E) is seen parked up in Pool Meadow bus station, Coventry, in September 1977. New in September 1969, she was allocated to Nuneaton garage before moving to Cradley Heath in May 1974. A move to Cannock came next in February 1977, before the Silver Jubilee livery, seen here, was applied in May. After that she was on a roving commission around the company's area, and even went on loan to Southdown Motor Services in June. After two more years at Cannock a move to Southgate Street, Leicester, came about, and in September 1981 she was transferred to Midland Red (East) together with her garage. She was withdrawn from here in September 1983. (Bernard Warr collection)

DD13 6210 stands in Pool Meadow bus station, Coventry, in 1974, after transfer to WMPTE the previous year. The new owners' painting priorities were clearly not the same as Midland Red's judging by the run-down look of the vehicle! From new she spent four years working from Digbeth, and after the transfer spent a further eight years at both Mosely Road and Coventry Road depots before withdrawal in 1981. (Bernard Warr collection)

DD13 6173 was new to Midland Red in July 1969 and was allocated initially to Tamworth, where she remained for nearly eight years. A move to Digbeth came in March 1977 with a return to Tamworth in June 1978. Upon the break-up of MROC, she became part of the Midland Red North fleet, remaining at Tamworth until she was withdrawn in October 1986. She is seen here in Tamworth on 19 August 1983. (Bernard Warr Collection)

LC10 6145 (SHA 645G), seen after withdrawal at the Wythall Transport Museum on 30 August 1999. New in 1969, she was an Oldbury garage vehicle for the first four years of her service life. She served time at Evesham, Cradley Heath and Digbeth garages before being loaned and then sold to City of Oxford Motor Services in 1978. Withdrawn in 1985, she moved straight into preservation. (Stuart Warr)

Former Stratford Blue 536 EUE, fleet number 2024, is seen working a service to Oxford in June 1971. 2024 was a Leyland Titan PD3/4 with Northern Counties seventy-three-seat bodywork, part of a batch of seven that were new in 1963. By the end of 1971 she had been sold to Isle of Man Road Services and was re-registered MN 57. In 1979 she was converted to open-top layout and ran in this form until early 1982. In May of that year she was purchased for preservation and is now with the Wirral Historical Transport Society. (Bernard Warr collection)

Former Stratford Blue GUE 2D, fleet number 2008, a Leyland Titan PD3A/1 with Willowbrook seventy-three-seat bodywork that was new in January 1966, is seen loading in Stratford for service 5 to Evesham in June 1971. After the merger with parent company Midland Red in January 1971, she remained working from Stratford garage until withdrawal in July 1972. She was purchased by Isle of Man Road Services in the following September and, after being re-registered MN 2671, remained in their service until September 1983. (Bernard Warr collection)

Former Stratford Blue 539 EUE, fleet number 2027, was a Leyland Titan PD3/4 with Northern Counties seventy-three-seat bodywork. New to Stratford Blue in January 1963, she was absorbed into the Midland Red fleet in January 1971. She is seen in June of that year preparing to leave Stratford on a service to Chipping Campden. However, she was not kept for long, being withdrawn in the following November and sold to Isle of Man Road Services. She entered service with them in January 1972, having been re-registered MN 60, and remained in use for a further nine years. (Bernard Warr collection)

LC12 6451 was one of the first batch delivered in May 1971 and was allocated to Bearwood garage for the first year. For the remainder of her eleven-year service life she was allocated to garages in the Leicester area. She has survived into preservation and is to be found at the Wythall Transport Museum. (Bernard Warr)

S25 6379 (YHA 379J) is seen leaving Stratford in the summer of 1971 on service 7 to Luxley. 6379 was almost new at this time and was based at Stratford garage after having spent two months at Ludlow when new in the previous January. (Bernard Warr collection)

On a beautiful day in May 1977, S25 (by then re-classified to F1) 6333 (YHA 333J) makes her way from Broadway to the tiny Cotswold village of Snowshill on service 400. 6333 was new in December 1970 with a Ford R192 chassis and Plaxton Derwent forty-five-seat body. She was allocated to Evesham garage at the time of this picture but had only a short service life, being withdrawn in February 1980. (Bernard Warr collection)

On the same beautiful May day in 1977, F1 6333 is seen arriving in the village of Snowshill, where passengers are already waiting. (Bernard Warr collection)

In April 1980, S26 6466 (DHA 466K) is seen making her way out of Burton-on-Trent, heading for Ashby-de-la-Zouch on service 704. Allocated to Swadlincote garage from new in 1972, this would have been a very regular turn. A transfer to Nuneaton garage occurred in October of 1980 and she was eventually withdrawn in May 1983. (Bernard Warr collection)

Stratford-upon-Avon bus station sees S26 6462 standing by for a run on service 519 to Leamington in August 1981. Her home garage was Leamington and had been for almost a year at this time. She was moved on to Rugby in May 1982. (Bernard Warr collection)

S26, 6467 (DHA 467K) was part of a batch of thirteen Leyland Leopard PSU3B/4Rs with Marshall fifty-three-seat bodywork that were delivered in the summer of 1972. 6467 was initially allocated to Ludlow depot in July 1972, but by February of the following year she was based at Swadlincote. This image was taken in June 1973, where she is seen working on the Birmingham to Derby 112 service. In July 1980 she was transferred to Nuneaton and, with the whole of that depot, became part of Midland Red South in September 1981. She was withdrawn from Nuneaton in March 1987. (Bernard Warr collection)

Dual-purpose S27 (note the coach seats) 234 (JHA 234L) is seen parked up in Cannock garage. The date is 12 September 1982, and although it does look as though there has been a frost, the white deposit is probably an anti-slip dressing to stop crews falling and injuring themselves. Cannock garage at this time was operated by Midland Red North and 234 was operated from here until withdrawn in October 1986. 234 is now preserved by Wyvern Omnibus Ltd of Stourport. (Bernard Warr collection)

S27 200 (JHA 200L) is seen in Coventry's Pool Meadow bus station on a dull November day in 1981. New to Midland Red in February 1973, she has now passed to Midland Red South and is working on service 657 to Nuneaton. (Bernard Warr collection)

The first N1, 101 (HHA 101L), is seen in the full Midland Red livery, as delivered in 1972. (Stuart Warr)

N1 101 was given an overall advertising livery in March 1974 and this was carried until a re-paint into NBC poppy red in April 1975. This photograph was taken in August 1974 after a transfer to Sandacre Street garage in Leicester, and she is seen in St Margaret's bus station on service 98 to Thurnby Lodge. (Bernard Warr collection)

Time has moved on, and in January 1985 N1 101 became the property of Midland Red West. For the last three months of 1988 she was on loan to Western National in Truro. On return she was converted to be a driver training vehicle, in which guise she operated for many years, as seen here outside Worcester garage on 28 December 2001. (Stuart Warr)

To celebrate the 100th anniversary of the founding of Midland Red, First Midland Red West restored 101 to her original livery. She is seen here at the Wythall Museum celebration on 31 July 2005. (Bernard Warr)

Ex-Midland Red D9 4981 loads passengers in Dudley bus station in September 1976. The sea of red buses that characterised Dudley for decades has been swept away by the march of time. (Chris Aston/Omnicolour)

After the WMPTE split, one of Sutton Coldfield's D9s is being towed along the Chester Road in Birmingham by the WTL tow truck in May 1976. The tow truck started life in 1956 as a D7 double-decker, 4531 (XHA 531), and spent most of her working life at Leamington garage until May 1971, when she moved to Digbeth. A year later she was converted to a recovery vehicle, painted all over yellow and retained at Digbeth using trade registration plate 070 HA. She was transferred to WMPTE on vesting day, 3 December 1973, allocated fleet no. 219 and stationed at Sutton Coldfield garage. The WMPTE trade plate 6178 O was used and she continued in this form until withdrawn in 1978. (Martin Llewellyn/Omnicolour)

Former Midland Red DD13 6215 (UHA 215H) heads along Navigation Street, Birmingham, en route to the bus station on service 114 from Sutton Coldfield in July 1975. New to Midland Red in October 1969, she became a Digbeth garage vehicle until the WMPTE vesting day, 3 December 1973, when she and twenty-five other DD13s were handed over to the new executive. She became a Sutton Coldfield vehicle and remained there until withdrawn in April 1981. The second doorway was removed in November 1975 and the seating capacity was increased by two. (Martin Llewellen/Omnicolour)

Former Midland Red S17 5469 (6469 HA), carrying full WTL livery, leaves Birmingham bus station on route 113 to Hardwick Arms in about May 1974. New to Worcester garage in January 1964, she transferred to Sutton in June 1967. On WMPTE vesting day, she, along with seventy-eight other S17s, was handed over to the PTE and based at Sutton Coldfield garage, from where she was working in the above picture. A move to Dudley came in July 1976, then to Stourbridge in February 1977, and she was withdrawn in April 1977. (Tony Thorne/ Omnicolour)

Former Midland Red S21 5853 (JHA 853E) discharges her passengers in Pool Meadow bus station, Coventry, after arriving from Birmingham on service 159 in October 1974. 5853 was new in March 1967 and spent all her service life with Midland Red, based at Bearwood garage. She was transferred to WMPTE on 3 December 1973 and was based at Mosely Road garage at the time of this picture. A move to Lea Hall garage came in November 1975 and final withdrawal came at the end of 1978. (Chris Aston/Omnicolour)

Former Midland Red S23 5981 (UHA 981H) is seen fully restored to the WMPTE livery that she carried between December 1973 and August 1980. She is seen here on 28 October 2001 at an open day organised by the Wythall Transport Museum. (Stuart Warr)

The business of G. Cooper & Sons of Oakengates was acquired on 15 October 1973 along with nine coaches and four buses. One of the coaches acquired from Coopers was this Bedford YRQ with forty-five-seat Duple Viceroy bodywork, which had been new to Coopers in December 1971. Registered WUX 656K, she was allocated a Midland Red fleet number of 2146 and based initially at Wellington depot. She was fitted for OMO in August 1975 and moved to Heath Hayes depot, where she is seen in the company of ex-Harpers Leyland Titan 2223. With the opening of the new Cannock depot in February 1977, she was transferred there with the remainder of the residents of Heath Hayes depot. Withdrawal came in the following July. (Bernard Warr collection)

Leyland National type N2 269 (NHA 269M) was part of the 1973 intake of fifty vehicles and was new in November 1973. For the first seven years of her service life she was based at Stafford depot; however, by November 1980, she had been moved to Banbury depot. Less than a year later, with the demise of MROC she became part of the Midland Red South fleet, remaining at Banbury depot, which also came under the new ownership. The 'all-over' advertising livery for National Travelworld, Banbury, was applied in February 1985 and was carried for about two years. This photograph was captured in June 1985 in Banbury. Further moves to Nuneaton, Leamington, Banbury (again) and finally Stratford came in quick succession. She was withdrawn from Stratford in May 1990 and was sold within a couple of months. (Bernard Warr collection)

In April 1974, Midland Red (MROC) took over the long-established business of Harper Brothers (Heath Hayes) Ltd and its subsidiary Tudor Rose Coaches of Sutton Coldfield. About fifty vehicles and the garage at Heath Hayes came with the takeover. Harper Bros NRF 349F is seen on 11 May 1974, before absorption into the Midland Red fleet the following September as fleet number 2223. She is a Leyland Titan PD3A/5 with a Northern Counties body, and was new in May 1968 as fleet number 23. She was operated by MROC until January 1977. (Bernard Warr collection)

Harper Bros 1294 RE, photographed on 20 August 1974 just prior to being taken over by MROC. A Guy Arab LUF with a Burlingham Seagull forty-two-seat body, she was new to Harpers in July 1959 and was given the fleet number 60. Although she was allocated a fleet number of 2260 by Midland Red, she was only operated for a month, being withdrawn in October 1974. (Bernard Warr collection)

Harper Bros SBF 217J, photographed in August 1974, just prior to the acquisition by MROC. A Leyland Leopard PSU3/3R with a Plaxton fifty-one-seat coach body, she was new to Harpers in October 1970 as their fleet number 78. After the takeover, fleet number 2278 was allocated and operation from Heath Hayes depot continued until she was transferred to the new Cannock depot in February 1977. At the end of 1977 ownership passed to National Travel (South West), but in March 1979 ownership was returned to MROC and 2278 became a Digbeth depot vehicle until she was withdrawn in January 1980. (Bernard Warr collection)

Former Harper Bros Daimler Fleetline CRG6LX 32 is seen in March 1975, after the takeover by Midland Red. She was new to Harpers in July 1971 and carried a Northern Counties seventy-five-seat body. Allocated initially to the Heath Hayes depot, number 2232 moved to the new Cannock depot when it opened in February 1977. She became a Midland Red (North) Ltd vehicle on that company's formation on 6 September 1981 and transferred to Shrewsbury garage. She was at Ludlow a year later and Shrewsbury garage from May 1983. She was withdrawn the following January. (Bernard Warr collection)

Part of a batch of fifty Leyland Leopard PSU3B/2R chassis with Marshall dual-purpose forty-nine-seat bodywork is 357 (GOH 357N). Classified by MROC as type S28 from new in November 1974, she was allocated to Digbeth depot until December 1979, when a move to Kidderminster took place. After MROC was broken up, 357 became part of the Midland Red West Fleet, based in Worcester. Withdrawal came in February 1990, as did a move into preservation. She is seen here at a rally to celebrate 100 years of Midland Red, which was held at the Wythall Transport Museum on 31 July 2005. (Bernard Warr)

Another image of preserved Midland Red S28 357 (GOH 357N), this time enjoying an outing in June 1997. (Bernard Warr collection)

Midland Red C18 674 (SOA 674S), a Leyland Leopard PSU3E/4R chassis with a Plaxton Supreme Express coach body, was new in January 1978 and allocated to Redditch depot. After a service life mostly with Midland Red West, she was withdrawn in March 1993 and entered preservation. She is seen in this image arriving at Kidderminster railway station on 11 October 1998. (Stuart Warr)

Leyland National N5 506 (JOX 506P) was one of the 1976 batch of thirty-four vehicles. Delivered in July of that year, she was allocated to Banbury depot and seated forty-nine passengers. She remained at Banbury after the formation of Midland Red South but was transferred to Rugby depot in September 1994, being withdrawn from there a year later. She was operated by the Birmingham Coach Co. Ltd from December 1995 to April 2002 as a driver training vehicle for part of the time, passing into preservation at that date. (Bernard Warr)

Leyland National 517 was also part of the 1976 batch of Nationals delivered to Midland Red in July of that year. However, by the time this photograph was taken on 22 June 1998, much water had gone under the bridge. Originally allocated to Shrewsbury depot, she passed to Midland Red North in 1981 but remained at Shrewsbury until April 1991, when a transfer to Tamworth took place, and then moved on to Cannock in May 1992. A Volvo engine was fitted in September 1993 and the roof pod was removed for use on service 825. At the same time the overall red livery seen here with 'Midland' branding was applied. A move to Stafford garage took place in May 1995 and she was finally withdrawn in September 2000 at the ripe old age of twenty-four! In this image she is seen in Pipers Row, Wolverhampton, setting out to return to Stafford. (Bernard Warr collection)

Photographed in August 1985, Leyland National 518 from the 1976 batch had a very different career from 517 above. Also allocated from new to Shrewsbury, she remained there for the whole of her service life until she was transferred to Cannock with serious accident damage in 1992, which resulted in her being scrapped. The high point of her career seems to have been this 'SAVERITE' all-over advertising livery, which was applied in March 1985 and carried until August 1988. (Bernard Warr collection)

Midland Red Leyland National N6 584 (NOE 584R), photographed shortly after being painted in a version of the Stratford Blue livery (and given the name *Rosemary*) in June 1990. There were seventy-five N6s introduced in 1976 and 1977, and 584 was delivered in February 1977 to Leamington garage, remaining there after the transfer to Midland Red South in 1981. A move to Stratford garage came in October 1989 and she was withdrawn in November 1991. Shortly afterwards a transfer to Cheltenham & Gloucester OC took place, and then in August 1995 a second transfer occurred, this time to Trent Motor Traction. She was finally withdrawn in May 2000. (Bernard Warr collection)

Seen in June 1985 in Victoria Road, Tamworth, with a terminating 110 service from Birmingham is Midland Red Leyland National type N7 617 (PUK 617R). New in March 1977 and allocated to Tamworth garage, she was transferred, with the garage, to Midland Red North in 1981. She gained this all-over advertising livery for the free *Tamworth Trader* in 1984 and retained it until she was transferred to Midland Red West in Worcester, where she was repainted in red and cream bus livery in November 1986. MRW allocated her to Digbeth depot and then to Redditch in February 1990. Withdrawn by MRW in May 1994, she passed to West Midlands Travel Ltd, Birmingham, and worked for them for a further three years. (Bernard Warr collection)

Midland Red N7 658 is captured entering Cheltenham on service 540 from Evesham on the afternoon of 11 June 1981. Note the final version of the NBC livery with full 'Wayfarer' branding. Three months after this picture was taken, Midland Red was broken down into six segments, and 658 was transferred to Midland Red West, complete with Evesham depot. (Bernard Warr collection)

Sixteen years after the previous image, 658 is pictured again, still working for MRW, in Abbey Road bus station, Evesham, on service 561 to Hampton. She carried on working for Evesham garage until January 2002, when she passed into preservation. She has been restored in the MRW livery, as seen here. (Bernard Warr collection)

The 1978 batch of Leyland Nationals comprised forty-two vehicles and they were given type code N8. 721 (WOC 721T), seen here, was new in September 1978 and was allocated to Bromsgrove depot. She passed to Midland Red West upon formation in September 1981 and worked from a variety of depots including Redditch, Digbeth and Worcester, arriving in April 1990 prior to this photograph being captured the following July. She was withdrawn in May 1995. (Bernard Warr collection)

The driver of Midland Red N9 758 (XOV 758T) has just boarded and is preparing to work service 316, Worcester–Hallow–Worcester, in June 2001. 758 was one of a batch of thirty-two buses supplied to Midland Red in September 1979. Originally allocated to Tamworth garage, she was operated by Midland Red North after the break-up of MROC. Five years later she was passed on to Midland Red West and worked from various garages, including Redditch, Evesham, Hereford and finally Worcester, as seen here. By this date Midland Red West had become First Midland Red and 758 soldiered on until the following November, when she was withdrawn after twenty-two years of service. (Bernard Warr collection)

Midland Red North adopted an all-over red livery based on a combination of earlier Midland Red styles. The first vehicle to be turned out in this livery was 969 (BVP 769V), photographed immediately after repairs to fire damage in September 1992 (the roof pod also disappeared during these repairs). 969 started life as 769 in November 1979 with Midland Red. She passed to Midland Red North in September 1981, continuing to be based at Wellington depot until a move to Cannock came in May 1991. Following the repairs, repainting and number change she moved to Stafford and remained there until she was withdrawn in April 1997. (Bernard Warr collection)

The final batch of Leyland Nationals purchased by Midland Red were a batch of twenty-five vehicles delivered in 1980 and 1981 with the type code N10. Part of this batch was 818 (BVP 818V), which was allocated to Nuneaton garage. She passed to Midland Red South with the depot in 1981 and remained there for the next fourteen years. After this she passed through C. & G. Coaches (Leamington) Ltd to Midland Red South ('Stagecoach Midland Red') in January 1996 and was allocated to Leamington depot, where she remained until withdrawn in February 1999. She is seen in Coventry in June 1981. (Bernard Warr collection)

For nearly three years, Midland Red North operated this MAN SG192 articulated bus with Göppel fifty-three-seat, sixty-seven-standing bodywork. A nearside view would show three sets of doors – one for entry and two for exiting the vehicle. She started life as a demonstrator, and after working for Midland Red Express and Midland Red West she came to Midland Red North in December 1983 and was allocated to Cannock garage. The red 'Chaserider' livery seen here was applied in February 1985 and she is seen the following month working an enthusiast special. Registered DAK 303V, she was given the MRN fleet number 1803. Withdrawn in February 1987, she was exported to Queensland, Australia, and was purchased by Marlin Coach Tours of Cairns. This operator removed the centre set of doors. (Bernard Warr collection)

Midland Red North 1801 (DAK 301V) was another of the ex-MAN demonstrators acquired by MRN in December 1983, after sessions with MREx and MRW. She was allocated to Cannock depot, given the 'Chaserider' overall red livery in June 1984, and was withdrawn in February 1987. She is seen working a shuttle service at the NEC on 18 October 1986. After a period in store she was sold to Marlin Coast Tours, Cairns, Queensland, Australia, in March 1987. As with 1803, Marlin removed the centre doors. (Bernard Warr collection)

Midland Red North 1504 (SND 301X) was a Leyland Leopard PSU5C/4R with Plaxton fifty-three-seat bodywork that was new to National Travel West in October 1981. Acquired by Midland Red North in June 1983, she carries both Mercian and Midland Express branding. 1504 is photographed on 27 July 1987 in Tamworth bus station, working the limited stop service X76 from Drayton Manor Park to Birmingham. 1504 was withdrawn in July 1989. (Bernard Warr collection)

Midland Red North 1527 (BPR 107Y) is seen working a Cannock to Lichfield service on 21 August 1996. The livery carried is the all-over red livery that was used on a number of MRN vehicles at about this time. 1527 was a Leyland Tiger TRCTL11/3R with a Duple Laser fifty-seat body and was new to Shamrock & Rambler, Bournemouth, in June 1983. She was acquired by MRN in January 1991 and, at the time of the photograph, had just been transferred to Tamworth depot. She was to remain there until withdrawn in November 1998. (Bernard Warr collection)

Midland Red North 1911 (B911 NBF) is seen in the summer of 1988, arriving at Drayton Manor Park with service X76. New to Midland Red North in November 1984, 1911 was a Leyland Olympian ONLXB/1R with Eastern Coach Works dual-purpose seventy-seat bodywork. The whole of her time with MRN was spent at Tamworth garage, from where she was withdrawn in March 1997. (Bernard Warr collection)

Sister to 1911, seen above, was 1912, seen here in Cannock bus station in July 1986. The Midland Express livery carried adorned all three of this batch of Leyland Olympians from new. 1912 was allocated to Cannock garage with a move to Tamworth in August 1988. She was withdrawn in August 1996. (Bernard Warr collection)

Seen in April 1987 is Midland Red North 81 (D81 CFA), a Ford Transit VE6 van chassis with Dormobile sixteen-seat bodywork. She was part of a batch of thirty vehicles that was purchased at the end of 1986 for a new network of minibus services in Walsall commencing on 26 January 1987. A new outstation was created in the town and all thirty vehicles were based there. Unfortunately, these services did not prove successful; all were withdrawn on 6 September 1987 and the outstation was closed. Along with other minibuses, 81 was transferred to Stafford depot and was one of twelve vehicles damaged or destroyed in the Stafford depot fire on 2 February 1992. (Bernard Warr collection)

Midland Red North 1747 (E27 UNE) is photographed leaving Birmingham on service 116 to Tamworth in May 1994. 1747 was a Leyland Tiger with Alexander N-type fifty-three-seat bodywork. She was new in March 1988 to Smith Shearing and joined the MRN fleet in October 1993, being allocated to Tamworth garage. Withdrawal came in June 2000. (Bernard Warr collection)

In April 1985, Midland Red Coaches acquired this 1984 Bova Europa from North Devon Ltd of Barnstaple. The registration was A 355 JJU and she was allocated fleet number 505. The following October she was renumbered 514, but by October 1986 she had been passed on to Milton Keynes Citi Bus Ltd. She is seen here in June 1985 turning right from the Digbeth dual carriageway into Rae Street to enter the Digbeth coach station. (Bernard Warr collection)

This is a picture of Midland Red Express fleet number 569 (A669 XDA), a Mercedes-Benz L508D with a Reeve Burgess nineteen-seat body. This was a single vehicle purchase and it was photographed shortly after delivery in March 1984, turning into Rae Street from Digbeth dual carriageway. When the lettering was placed on this attractive version of the traditional Midland Red coach livery, it proclaimed that it was a 'Midland Red Mini Cruiser'. With the merger of Midland Red Express and Midland Red West in December 1986, she became part of the combined fleet and was given fleet number 1405. She remained operational with MRW, wearing various liveries, until November 1995. (Bernard Warr collection)

Midland Red Coaches fleet number 1019 was a Leyland Tiger with Duple Caribbean fifty-seat coachwork, and is seen here in June 1988 after she had acquired the National Express coach livery in April the previous year (and lost two seats to become a forty-eight-seater). She was new to Midland Red Express in December 1984 as fleet number 568 and carried National Holidays livery. With the merger of MRExp and MRW in December 1986 she became part of the combined fleet but remained at Digbeth depot until November 1995, when a transfer to Redditch took place. She was withdrawn about a year later and passed to Western National in Truro, but was never operated by that company. (Bernard Warr collection)

Midland Red South 955 (BHL 622K) is seen in May 1995 at Nuneaton depot. A Daimler Fleetline with Northern Counties seventy-six-seat bodywork, she was new to West Riding Automobile Co. Ltd, Wakefield, in February 1972 and passed to MRS thirteen years later. Her stay was a relatively short one as she was withdrawn in July 1987. (Bernard Warr collection)

Photographed in June 1985 is XCK 221R, a Leyland Leopard PSU5B/4R with Willowbrook fifty-one-seat bodywork that was new to National Travel West in May 1977 and passed to Ribble Motor Services in Preston seven years later. After only a year she was purchased by MRS, given fleet number 90 and allocated to Rugby depot. After two years there she was moved to Nuneaton depot for another two-year stint, before passing to Stratford depot, from where she was withdrawn in June 1989. (Bernard Warr collection)

Just up from the Bancroft Basin canal and river interchange is High Street, Stratford-upon-Avon. On a busy day in July 1996 Midland Red South 979 (SCN 281S) is seen pulling away from the bus stop adjacent to the Encore Pub and restaurant on service 215 to Bidford. 979 was a Leyland Atlantean with Alexander bodywork, new to Tyne & Wear PTE in July 1978. She was purchased by Midland Red South in January 1996 and remained with the company for the next three years. (Bernard Warr collection)

Midland Red South 1 (420 GAC) was a Leyland Tiger with Plaxton Paramount forty-nine-seat coach bodywork that was new to MRS in August 1983 and based at Rugby depot. She was initially registered as A190 GVC but was re-registered to 420 GAC in April 1988. In May 1985, a toilet was provided and four seats were removed to make space for it. In May 1990, she was transferred to Banbury depot, from where she was working when photographed in March 1992 in Sheffield bus station on a Poole to Leeds National Express Coach service. Just over a year later she acquired a third registration, becoming A75 NAC. After eight years at Banbury depot she was transferred to Stratford in April 1998, from where she was withdrawn in January 1999. (Bernard Warr collection)

A further incarnation of Midland Red South 1, showing the post-National Express livery and the new registration, A75 NAC. (Bernard Warr collection)

Midland Red West Leyland National 179 is seen in St Peter's Square, Hereford, in July 1985 working town service H27. Built as a dual-door bus when new to Northern General in August 1973, one doorway was removed by that operator in December 1980. After briefly working for Midland Red South for three months from May 1984, she joined the MRW fleet in August 1984 and took up residence at Hereford garage. The rest of her service life was to be spent there and she was sold for scrap in December 1989. (Bernard Warr collection)

Photographed in June 1988 is Midland Red West 1072 (PCW 672P), a Leyland Leopard PSU3C/4R with a Duple coach body that was new to Ribble Motor Services Ltd in March 1976. She was acquired by MRW in March 1985 and, after being fitted with OMO equipment, entered service in May. On delivery she was carrying the National Express all-over white livery, but in May 1987 she was repainted into the yellow and red Midland Express livery seen here. She was withdrawn at the end of 1989. (Bernard Warr collection)

It was quite common for vehicles to enter a second 'career' after their public service days were over. NOE 614R is a typical example. New in 1976 as Midland Red C17 fleet number 614 (Leyland Leopard PSU3D/4R with Plaxton Supreme bodywork), she passed to Midland Red Express Ltd at formation in September 1981 and to Midland Red West upon merger with MRE Ltd in December 1986. She was withdrawn in March 1991, but by April 1997 she had been converted into a tow truck and painted in all-over yellow, as seen here on 17 December 1998, based at Worcester garage. She continued in this role until withdrawal in December 2010. (Stuart Warr)

Leyland National Mk I AFJ 755T, with First Midland Red fleet number 755, is seen outside Evesham garage on 5 December 1998. Originally owned by Western National OC Ltd from new in April 1979, she was acquired by Midland Red West in November 1989 and remained with the company until November 2000. (Stuart Warr)

One of the many second-hand Leyland Nationals acquired by MRW is this Mk II, BOU 8V, fleet number 908. Built originally for the Bristol Omnibus Co., she entered service in September 1980. She was passed on to Badgerline, Weston-super-Mare, in September 1986, South Wales Transport Co. Ltd in August 1998 and to First Midland Red in August 1999. She was based at Worcester garage, which is where she was photographed on 28 December 2001 and from where she was withdrawn in May 2002. (Stuart Warr)

Photographed on 17 December 1998 outside Evesham garage, fleet number 867 (HUA 607Y) was acquired by Midland Red West from Yorkshire Rider the previous April. Prior to that, she had spent the first five years of her service life with the West Yorkshire PTE. She worked initially from Evesham garage, still in 'Calderline' livery until July 1998, when she gained the MRW standard livery of red and cream. A move to Worcester came in January 2001, but the following November an expensive engine rebuild became necessary and she was placed in store. She was sold for scrap in August 2004. (Stuart Warr)

Midland Red West 1006 (B106 JAB), a Leyland Tiger TRCTL11/3RH chassis with a Plaxton Paramount II forty-seven-seat coach body, was new to MRW in April 1985, based at Worcester depot. During its service life, it has carried several different liveries including the silver and green 'Eurocruiser' from April to December 1985; white, maroon and gold 'Midwest' to May 1987; National Express all-over white 'Rapide' to January 1993 and overall red coach livery with 'Midland Red Coaches' branding changed to 'First Midland Red' from then on. She worked from Hereford, Digbeth, Evesham and Worcester depots before being withdrawn in April 2006, and is seen here on 5 December 1998 outside Evesham garage, where she was based at that time. She is now preserved in overall white livery. (Stuart Warr)

Seen at the Worcester garage is Midland Red West minibus 1310 (C310 PNP), a Mercedes-Benz L608D with a twenty-seat PMT minibus conversion. She was new in November 1985 as part of a batch of sixty similar vehicles introduced to a new network of local services in Worcester. Using the 'Citibus' branding, they became a familiar sight to the Worcester traveller. This picture dates from 17 December 1998, when the branding had been removed ready for export to Trinidad and Tobago, where she arrived at the end of that year. (Stuart Warr)

Midland Red West 1422 (E422 KUY), seen in West Bromwich Queen Square, was a Mercedes-Benz 609D with a twenty-seat Reeve Burges minibus conversion. Twenty-six examples entered service at Hereford garage on 23 April 1988 in a yellow, green and orange 'Hereford Hopper' livery for use on local Hereford services. Although retaining the livery by the time of this photograph, 1422 had moved to Digbeth garage in April 1991 and the livery was changed to the standard red and cream by September 1994. A further move to Kidderminster took place in October 1995 and after six years of service there, she was withdrawn in October 2001. (Bernard Warr collection)

Seen on 5 December 1998 parked outside Worcester garage is Midland Red West 807 (E807 MOU), a thirty-one-seat Mercedes-Benz 811D with Optare StarRider bodywork. Previously owned by both Badgerline of Weston-super-Mare and Western National in Truro, this 1988 vehicle arrived at MRW Worcester garage in February 1997, gaining the red and cream livery in April of that year. She was withdrawn from Hereford garage in August 2002. (Stuart Warr)

A Midland Red West Leyland Lynx with forty-nine-seat Lynx integral bodywork, 1104 (G104 HNP) is seen parked up in Bridgnorth after working there on service 436 from Shrewsbury in October 1994. 1104 was part of a batch of fifty vehicles suppled to MRW in March 1990 for use at Digbeth depot. By the time of this photograph she had moved on to Kidderminster depot. She was withdrawn from Redditch depot in February 2005. (Bernard Warr collection)

A Midland Red West Leyland Lynx with forty-nine-seat Lynx integral bodywork, 1131 (G131 HNP) is seen in West Bromwich Queen Square in the summer of 1991. 1131 was part of a batch of fifty vehicles suppled to MRW in March 1990 for use at Digbeth depot. In April 1994, she moved to Redditch depot and spent the rest of her MRW service life there, being withdrawn in May 2004. She was passed to Leicester Citybus Ltd ('First Leicester') and was scrapped from there with fire damage in June 2006. (Bernard Warr collection)

Midland Red West Leyland Lynx 1147 (G147 HNP) is seen picking up passengers in Mill Street, Ludlow, adjacent to the town's market. The date would have be some time in the summer of 1994. At this time 1147 was a Kidderminster depot vehicle. (Bernard Warr collection)

Midland Red West Dennis Lance 203 (L203 AAB) stands in Bilston after working service 401. She was part of a batch of thirty-seven similar vehicles supplied to Digbeth depot in 1994 to replace the Leyland Lynx fleet that had heralded a Midland Red successor's return to 'Black Country' services. Fitted with Plaxton Verde forty-nine-seat bodies, they remained at Digbeth until closure of the depot in April 1997. Note the Badgerline symbol on the lower rear quarter panel, signifying the merger between Badgerline and MRW. (Bernard Warr collection)

Seen outside Evesham depot on 17 December 1998 is Midland Red West 244 (M244 MRW) – note the use of personalised registration numbers! A Dennis Lance with Plaxton Verde forty-nine-seat bodywork, she was part of a batch of nineteen vehicles delivered in the summer of 1995. Allocated initially to Worcester depot in July 1995, she was to remain there until January 2006, when a move to Kidderminster took place. She passed to the Diamond Bus Co. Ltd with the assets and operations of Kidderminster in March 2013. (Stuart Warr)

A Dennis Lance with Plaxton Verde forty-nine-seat bodywork new to Plaxton in September 1996. However, because of warranty work that Plaxtons were obliged to do to vehicles 201 to 256, this vehicle was placed on long-term loan to MRW and was based at Worcester depot from October 1996 until January 2000. The registration number was P453 BPH and she was allocated fleet number 257. As can be seen from the image, the MRW livery of red and cream was only applied to the front of the vehicle, the remainder staying in 'dealer' white. 257 was photographed outside Evesham garage on 17 December 1998. (Stuart Warr)

Minibus 527 (S527 RWP) was one of sixty-four Mercedes-Benz 0814 Vario minibuses with Plaxton Beaver II twenty-two-seat bodywork that were introduced to Midland Red West's Worcester depot in August 1998. In this photograph she is seen in Worcester bus station, ready to work on service 28, about a year later. In November 2004, she and forty-two others of the batch passed to First Devon & Cornwall in Plymouth. (Bernard Warr collection)